STEP-BY-STEP

Thai Cooking

STEP-BY-STEP

Thai Cooking

CAROL BOWEN

SHOOTING STAR PRESS

This edition printed in 1995 for:
Shooting Star Press Inc
230 Fifth Avenue – Suite 1212
New York, NY 10001

Shooting Star Press books are available at special discounts for bulk purchases for sales promotions, premiums, fund-raising, or educational use. Special edition or book excerpts can also be created to specification. For details contact: Special Sales Director, Shooting Star Press Inc., 230 Fifth Avenue, Suite 1212, New York, NY 10001

© Parragon Book Service Ltd 1994

ISBN 1 56924 186 X

Printed in Italy

Acknowledgements:

Design & DTP: Pedro & Frances Prá-Lopez / Kingfisher Design
Art Direction: Clive Hayball
Managing Editor: Alexa Stace
Special Photography: Martin Brigdale
Home Economist: Jill Eggleton
Step-by-Step Photography: Karl Adamson
Step-by-Step Home Economist: Joanna Craig
Stylist: Helen Trent

Food kindly supplied by B E International Foods Ltd
Photographs on pages 6, 18, 28, 52 & 64: By courtesy of ZEFA

Contents

CHAPTER ONE

Appetizers

From the spicy exuberance of a hot-and-sour duck salad to the more subtle flavors of a chicken or beef satay, the importance of the appetizer-style dish has long been recognized and celebrated in Thai households. Unlike Western cuisine, however, a Thai appetizer is most likely to be served before a meal with drinks, as a snack between meals, as party or celebration food, or as a dish that is served just before and then with the main course.

Typically several dishes of this type are served at once in the age-old tradition of enticing and tempting the appetite or teasing the palate. In the pages that follow, you will find a selection that includes baby fish cakes with a cucumber garnish; tiny skewered chicken or beef kebabs called satay that are served with a flavorsome peanut sauce; a colorful array of crisp vegetable crudités served with a Thai shrimp dipping sauce; and mouthwatering hot-and-sour or sweet-and-sour crisp salad mixtures.

Fortunately for the cook these are dishes that can be prepared well ahead of time or can be assembled and cooked very quickly. Consider, too, some of the main-course recipes in bite-sized portions – Bangkok Barbecued Chicken Legs and Duckling with Ginger and Lime Dressing double up beautifully as appetizer or main course fare.

Opposite: *The fishing fleet returns at sunset to Kata Beach, Phuket.*

RED CURRY FISH CAKES

Just the thing to entice the tastebuds, Thai fish cakes make a delicious appetizer and good introduction to a Thai-style meal. Almost any kind of fish fillets or seafood can be used.

STEP 2

MAKES ABOUT 24 (TO SERVE 4-6)

2 lb fish fillets or prepared seafood, such as
  cod, haddock, shrimp, crabmeat or lobster
1 egg, beaten
2 tbsp chopped fresh cilantro
Red Curry Paste (see page 30)
1 bunch scallions, finely chopped
vegetable oil, for deep-frying
chili flowers, to garnish

CUCUMBER SALAD:
1 large cucumber, peeled and grated
2 shallots, peeled and grated
2 red chilies, seeded and very finely chopped
2 tbsp fish sauce
2 tbsp dried powdered shrimp
1¹/₂-2 tbsp lime juice

1 Place the fish in a blender or food processor with the egg, cilantro, and curry paste and purée until smooth and well blended.

2 Turn the mixture into a bowl, add the scallions and mix well to combine.

3 Using 2 tablespoons of the fish mixture at a time, shape it into balls, then flatten them slightly with your fingers to make fish cakes.

4 Heat the oil in a wok or saucepan until hot, add a few of the fish cakes and deep-fry for a few minutes until brown and cooked through. Remove with a slotted spoon and drain on paper towels. Keep warm while cooking the remaining fish cakes.

5 Meanwhile, to make the cucumber salad, mix the cucumber with the shallots, chilies, fish sauce, dried shrimp, and lime juice.

6 Serve the salad immediately with the warm fish cakes.

STEP 3

STEP 4

CHILIES

When handling chilies be very careful not to touch your face or eyes. Chili juice is a powerful irritant, and can be very painful on the skin. Always wash your hands after preparing chilies.

STEP 5

CRUDITES WITH SHRIMP SAUCE

This is a classic Thai appetizer – fruit and vegetable crudités served with a spicy, garlicky shrimp sauce. It is served at almost every meal, and each family has their own favorite recipe.

STEP 1

SERVES 6

about 1½ lb prepared raw fruit and
vegetables, such as broccoli, cauliflower,
apple, pineapple, cucumber, celery, bell
peppers and mushrooms

SAUCE:
2 oz dried shrimp
½-in cube shrimp paste
3 garlic cloves, crushed
4 red chilies, seeded and chopped
6 stems fresh cilantro, coarsely chopped
juice of 2 limes
fish sauce, to taste
brown sugar, to taste

Note: Although easy to make, the sauce
is prepared at least 12 hours before
serving.

1 Soak the dried shrimp in warm
water for 10 minutes.

2 To make the sauce, place the
shrimp paste, drained shrimp,
garlic, chilies, and cilantro in a food
processor or blender and process until
well chopped but not smooth.

3 Turn the sauce mixture into a bowl
and add the lime juice, mixing well.

4 Add the fish sauce and brown
sugar to taste to the sauce, mixing
to blend well. Cover the bowl tightly and
chill the sauce in the refrigerator for at
least 12 hours, or overnight.

5 To serve, arrange the fruit and
vegetables attractively on a large
serving plate. Place the prepared sauce in
the center for dipping.

STEP 2

STEP 3

STEP 4

ALTERNATIVE

Hard-boiled quail eggs are often added to
this traditional fruit and vegetable platter,
and certainly would be offered on a
special occasion.

SWEET-&-SOUR TOFU SALAD

Tofu or bean curd is a delicious, healthy alternative to meat. Mixed with a variety of crisp stir-fried vegetables, then tossed in a piquant sweet-and-sour dressing, it makes an ideal light meal or appetizer.

STEP 2

STEP 3

STEP 4

STEP 5

SERVES 4-6

2 tbsp vegetable oil
1 tbsp sesame oil
1 garlic clove, crushed
1 lb firm tofu, cubed
1 onion, sliced
1 carrot, cut into julienne strips
1 stalk celery, sliced
2 small red bell peppers, cored, seeded and sliced
1½ cups snow peas, trimmed and halved
1 cup broccoli flowerets
1 cup thin green beans, halved
2 tbsp oyster sauce
1 tbsp tamarind concentrate
1 tbsp fish sauce
1 tbsp tomato paste
1 tbsp light soy sauce
1 tbsp chili sauce
2 tbsp sugar
1 tbsp white-wine vinegar
pinch of ground star anise
1 tsp cornstarch
1¼ cups water

1 Heat the vegetable oil in a large, heavy-based skillet or wok until hot. Add the crushed garlic and cook for a few seconds.

2 Add the tofu in batches and stir-fry over a gentle heat until golden on all sides. Remove with a slotted spoon and keep warm.

3 Add the onion, carrot, celery, red bell pepper, snow peas, broccoli, and green beans to the pan and stir-fry for about 2-3 minutes or until tender-crisp.

4 Add the oyster sauce, tamarind concentrate, fish sauce, tomato paste, soy sauce, chili sauce, sugar, vinegar, and star anise, mixing well to blend. Stir-fry for a further 2 minutes.

5 Mix the cornstarch with the water, then add to the pan with the fried tofu. Stir-fry gently until the sauce boils and thickens slightly.

6 Serve the salad immediately on warm plates.

STEP 1

STEP 2

STEP 3

STEP 5

CHICKEN OR BEEF SATAY

A favorite Thai dish made with tender chicken or beef and served with a spicy peanut sauce.

SERVES 4-6

4 boneless, skinned chicken breast halves or
   1½ lb sirloin steak, trimmed

MARINADE:
1 small onion, finely chopped
1 garlic clove, crushed
1-in piece gingerroot, peeled and grated
2 tbsp dark soy sauce
2 tsp chili powder
1 tsp ground cilantro
2 tsp dark brown sugar
1 tbsp lemon or lime juice
1 tbsp vegetable oil

SAUCE:
1¼ cups coconut milk
⅓ cup crunchy peanut butter
1 tbsp fish sauce
1 tsp lemon or lime juice
salt and pepper

1 Trim any fat from the chicken or beef, then cut it into thin strips, about 3 in long.

2 To make the marinade, place all the ingredients in a shallow non-metallic dish and mix well. Add the chicken or beef strips and turn in the marinade until well coated. Cover and leave to marinate for 2 hours or overnight in the refrigerator.

3 Remove the meat from the marinade and thread the pieces, concertina style, onto bamboo or thin wooden skewers.

4 Broil the chicken and beef satays for 8-10 minutes, turning and brushing occasionally with the marinade, until cooked through.

5 Meanwhile, to make the sauce, mix the coconut milk with the peanut butter, fish sauce, and lemon juice in a saucepan. Bring to a boil, then cook for 3 minutes. Season to taste and serve with the cooked satays.

SATAY STICKS

Fine bamboo or wooden skewers are traditionally used to cook satays. Soak them in cold water for at least 1 hour before using to prevent them from burning and scorching during cooking.

HOT-&-SOUR DUCK SALAD

A refreshing, tangy salad, drizzled with a lime juice and Thai fish sauce dressing. It makes a splendid appetizer or light main course dish.

STEP 1

STEP 2

STEP 3

STEP 4

SERVES 4

2 heads crisp salad lettuce, washed and
  separated into leaves
2 shallots, thinly sliced
4 scallions, chopped
1 celery stalk, finely sliced into julienne
  strips
2 in piece cucumber, cut into julienne strips
1 cup bean sprouts
1 x 7-oz can water chestnuts, drained and
  sliced
4 duck breast fillets, roasted and sliced (see
  page 43)
orange slices, to serve

DRESSING:
3 tbsp fish sauce
1½ tbsp lime juice
2 garlic cloves, crushed
1 red chili pepper, seeded and very finely
  chopped
1 green chili pepper, seeded and very finely
  chopped
1 tsp palm or dark brown sugar

1 Mix the lettuce leaves with the shallots, scallions, celery, cucumber, bean sprouts and water chestnuts. Place the mixture on a large serving platter.

2 Arrange the duck breast slices on top of the salad in an attractive, overlapping pattern.

3 To make the dressing, put the fish sauce, lime juice, garlic, chilies and sugar into a small saucepan. Heat gently, stirring constantly. Taste and adjust the piquancy if liked by adding more lime juice, or add more fish sauce to reduce the sharpness.

4 Drizzle the warm salad dressing over the duck salad and serve immediately.

JULIENNE STRIPS

To cut vegetables into julienne strips, first slice them thinly into even-sized slices. Stack the slices on top of each other, then cut with a sharp knife into very thin shreds.

CHAPTER TWO

Fish & Shellfish

It is not surprising that fish and shellfish feature prominently on the typical Thai menu, so much of the country is surrounded by water. Whole fresh fish are often simply charcoal-grilled, steamed, fried or baked. Many are baked in banana leaves to keep the flesh moist and succulent. Seafood is often skewered and barbecued or sizzled in a wok with rice, chilies, nuts and finely sliced or diced vegetables to make a quick, delicious one-pot meal. Both fish and seafood are also given the pungent-flavored treatment in a whole host of curries from mild and mellow to fiery and fierce. Fruit such as pineapple, papaya and mango may also be added to give a flavor and texture contrast.

Whatever the fish, the golden rule is to choose seafood that is absolutely at the peak of freshness. Look for whole fish that has bright eyes, red gills, firm flesh, shiny scales and a fresh sealike odor. Never settle for second best! Likewise choose shellfish that is still tightly locked and closed in its shell. Discard those that are already open and do not close if sharply tapped.

Opposite: *Fishing boats moored on Chon Khram beach, Koh Samui Island. The seas around Thailand teem with fish of every kind.*

STEP 1

STEP 2

STEP 3

STEP 4

FRIED RICE & SHRIMP

When you've got one eye on the clock and a meal to make, this is the one! Made in a flash, yet simply stunning to look at, its taste belies its simplicity.

SERVES 4

¼ cup butter
3 tbsp vegetable oil
3 cups cooked basmati rice
6 scallions, finely sliced
1 cup snow peas, halved
1 carrot, cut into fine julienne strips
¾ cup canned water chestnuts, drained and
    sliced
salt and pepper
1 small crisp lettuce, shredded
12 oz raw, shelled jumbo shrimp or tiger
    prawns
1 large red chili, seeded and sliced diagonally
3 egg yolks
4 tsp sesame oil

1 Heat the butter and the oil in a large, heavy-based skillet or wok. Add the cooked rice and stir-fry for 2 minutes.

2 Add the scallions, snow peas, carrot, water chestnuts and salt and pepper to taste, mixing well. Stir-fry over medium heat for 2 minutes longer.

3 Add the shredded lettuce, shrimp and chili and stir-fry for a further 2 minutes.

4 Beat the egg yolks with the sesame oil and stir into the pan, coating the rice and vegetable mixture. Stir-fry for about 2 minutes to set the egg mixture.

5 Serve the rice and shrimp at once on warmed plates.

FRIED RICE

For perfect fried rice, it is best to cook the rice ahead of time and allow it to cool completely before adding it to the hot oil. That way the rice grains will remain separate, and the rice will not become lumpy or heavy.

SIZZLED CHILI SHRIMP

Another Thai classic – jumbo shrimp marinated in a chili-flavored mixture, then stir-fried with cashews. Serve with a fluffy rice and braised vegetables.

STEP 1

SERVES 4

5 tbsp soy sauce
5 tbsp dry sherry
3 dried red chilies, seeded and chopped
2 garlic cloves, crushed
2 tsp grated gingerroot
5 tbsp water
1¼ lb raw, shelled jumbo shrimp or tiger prawns
1 large bunch scallions, chopped
²/₃ cup salted cashew nuts
3 tbsp vegetable oil
2 tsp cornstarch

1 Mix the soy sauce with the sherry, chilies, garlic, ginger and water in a large bowl.

2 Add the shrimp or prawns, scallions and cashews and mix well. Cover tightly and leave to marinate for at least 2 hours, stirring occasionally.

3 Heat the oil in a large, heavy-based skillet or wok. Drain the shrimp, scallions and cashews from the marinade with a slotted spoon and add to the skillet, reserving the marinade. Stir-fry over a high heat for 1-2 minutes.

4 Mix the reserved marinade with the cornstarch, then add to the skillet and stir-fry for about 30 seconds until the marinade forms a slightly thickened shiny glaze over the shrimp mixture.

5 Serve the shrimp immediately, with rice.

STEP 2

STEP 3

VARIATION

For an attractive presentation, serve this dish on mixed wild rice and basmati or other long-grain rice. Start cooking the wild rice in salted boiling water. After 10 minutes, add the basmati or other rice and continue boiling until all grains are tender. Drain well and adjust the seasoning.

STEP 4

STEP 1

STEP 2a

STEP 2b

STEP 3

PINEAPPLE & FISH CURRY

This is a fiery hot Thai curry dish that is all the better for serving with refreshing (and cooling) fresh pineapple pieces.

SERVES 4

2 pineapples
3-in piece galangal, sliced
2 blades of lemongrass, bruised and then
    chopped
5 sprigs fresh basil
1 lb firm white fish fillets, cubed (monkfish,
    halibut or cod, for example)
4 oz raw, shelled shrimp
2 tbsp vegetable oil
2 tbsp Red Curry Paste (see page 30)
1/2 cup thick coconut milk or cream
2 tbsp fish sauce
2 tsp palm or dark brown sugar
2-3 red chilies, seeded and cut into thin
    julienne strips
about 6 kaffir lime leaves, torn into pieces
cilantro sprigs, to garnish

1 Cut the pineapples in half lengthwise. Remove the flesh, reserving the shells if using (see box). Remove the core from the pineapple flesh, then dice into bite-sized pieces.

2 Place the galangal in a large shallow saucepan with the lemongrass and basil. Add the fish cubes and just enough water to cover. Bring to a boil, reduce the heat and simmer for about 2 minutes. Add the shrimp and cook for a further 1 minute or until the fish is just cooked. Remove from the flavored stock with a slotted spoon and keep warm.

3 Heat the oil in another heavy-based pot or wok. Add the curry paste and cook for 1 minute. Stir in the coconut milk or cream, fish sauce, brown sugar, chilies and lime leaves.

4 Add the pineapple and cook until just heated through. Add the cooked fish and mix gently to combine.

5 Spoon into the reserved pineapple shells, if liked, and serve immediately, garnished with sprigs of cilantro.

VARIATION

This dish could be served on plates, but for a stunning presentation on a special occasion, serve in the hollowed-out shells of the pineapple.

WRAPPED FISH WITH GINGER

This is fish cooked in a healthy, palate-tingling way. Whole mackerel or trout are stuffed with herbs, wrapped in foil or, more authentically, banana leaves, baked and then drizzled with a fresh ginger butter.

STEP 1

SERVES 4
OVEN: 375°F

8 oz whole trout or mackerel, dressed
4 tbsp chopped fresh cilantro
5 garlic cloves, crushed
2 tsp grated lemon or lime rind
salt and pepper
2 tsp vegetable oil
banana leaves, for wrapping (optional)
6 tbsp butter
1 tbsp grated gingerroot
1 tbsp light soy sauce
cilantro sprigs and lemon or lime wedges, to
    garnish

1 Wash and dry the fish. Mix the cilantro with the garlic, lemon or lime rind and salt and pepper to taste. Spoon into the fish cavities.

2 Brush the fish with a little oil, season well and place each fish on a double thickness sheet of baking parchment or foil and wrap up well to enclose. Alternatively, wrap in banana leaves (see right).

3 Place on a baking tray and bake in the preheated oven for about 25 minutes or until the flesh will flake easily.

4 Meanwhile, melt the butter in a small saucepan. Add the grated ginger and stir until well mixed, then stir in the soy sauce.

5 To serve, unwrap the fish packages, drizzle the ginger butter over and garnish with cilantro and lemon or lime wedges.

STEP 2a

STEP 2b

BANANA LEAVES

For a really authentic touch, wrap the fish in banana leaves, which can be ordered from specialist Oriental supermarkets. They are not edible, but impart a delicate flavor to the fish.

STEP 3

CHAPTER THREE

Meat & Poultry

Unlike many other Oriental nationalities, the Thais are not restricted by religion over what they can eat, so pork, beef and lamb appear with poultry on the menu. However, since quantities can be scarce by Western standards, the Thais invent imaginative dishes that cunningly stretch limited supplies to the full.

Hence you will find wonderful meats stretched with noodles, chicken stir-fried with an array of vegetables, beef extended with glistening shredded bok choy cabbage, and meats simmered and stretched with vegetables in a coconut milk and chili paste sauce.

In this chapter you'll also find some old favorites with the Thai inspirational twist – chicken roasted with the addition of lemongrass, kaffir lime leaves, ginger, cilantro and garlic; and fried beef steak, the steak cut into strips and stir-fried with colored bell peppers, scallions, celery, mushrooms, onions and crunchy cashew nuts, all the better for serving with a mound of fluffy rice and a few braised vegetables.

Opposite: *Every imaginable kind of foodstuff is for sale in this floating market at Damnoen Saduak, south of Bangkok.*

STEP 3a

STEP 3b

STEP 4

STEP 5

RED CHICKEN CURRY

The chicken is cooked with a curry paste made from red chilies (see below). It is a fiery hot sauce – for a milder version, reduce the number of chilies used.

SERVES 6

4 tbsp vegetable oil
2 garlic cloves, crushed
1³/₄ cups coconut milk
6 chicken breast fillets, skinned and cut into
    bite-sized pieces
¹/₂ cup chicken stock
2 tbsp fish sauce
kaffir lime leaves, sliced red chilies and
    chopped cilantro, to garnish

RED CURRY PASTE:
8 dried red chilies, seeded and chopped
1-in piece galangal or gingerroot, peeled and
    sliced
3 stalks lemongrass, chopped
1 garlic clove, peeled
2 tsp shrimp paste
1 kaffir lime leaf, chopped
1 tsp ground cilantro
³/₄ tsp ground cumin
1 tbsp chopped fresh cilantro
1 tsp salt and black pepper

1 To make the curry paste, place all the ingredients in a food processor or blender and process until smooth.

2 Heat the oil in a large, heavy-based saucepan or wok. Add the garlic and cook until it turns golden.

3 Stir in the curry paste and cook for 10-15 seconds, then gradually add the coconut milk, stirring constantly (don't worry if the mixture starts to look curdled at this stage).

4 Add the chicken pieces and turn in the sauce mixture to coat. Cook gently for about 3-5 minutes or until almost tender.

5 Stir in the chicken stock and fish sauce, mixing well, then cook for a further 2 minutes.

6 Transfer to a warmed serving dish and garnish with lime leaves, sliced red chilies and chopped cilantro. Serve with rice.

CURRY PASTE

There are two basic curry pastes used in Thai cuisine – red and green, depending upon whether they are made from red or green chili peppers. The basic paste can be made and stored in a covered jar in the refrigerator for up to 2 weeks.

STEP 2

STEP 3

STEP 4

STEP 5

BARBECUED CHICKEN LEGS

Just the thing to put on the barbecue – chicken legs, coated with a spicy, curry-like butter, then grilled until crispy and golden. Serve with a crisp green seasonal salad and rice.

SERVES 6

12 chicken drumsticks

SPICED BUTTER:
³/₄ cup butter, softened
2 garlic cloves, crushed
1 tsp grated gingerroot
2 tsp ground turmeric
4 tsp cayenne pepper
2 tbsp lime juice
3 tbsp mango chutney

1 Prepare a barbecue with medium coals or preheat a conventional broiler to moderate.

2 To make the Spiced Butter mixture, beat the butter with the garlic, ginger, turmeric, cayenne pepper, lime juice and chutney until it is blended well.

3 Using a sharp knife, slash each chicken leg to the bone 3-4 times.

4 Cook the drumsticks over the barbecue for about 12-15 minutes or until almost cooked. Alternatively, broil the chicken for about 10-12 minutes until almost cooked, turning halfway through.

5 Spread the chicken legs liberally with the butter mixture and continue to cook for a further 5-6 minutes, turning and basting frequently with the butter until golden and crisp.

6 Serve hot or cold with a crisp green salad and rice.

VARIATION

This spicy butter mixture would be equally effective on grilled chicken or turkey breast fillets. Skin before coating with the mixture.

STEP 2

STEP 3

STEP 5a

STEP 5b

ROAST BABY CHICKEN

Baby chicken, stuffed with lemongrass and lime leaves, coated with a spicy Thai paste, then roasted until crisp and golden, make a wonderful, aromatic dish for a special occasion.

SERVES 4
OVEN: 400°F

*4 baby chicken weighing about 12 oz-1 lb
   each
cilantro leaves and lime wedges, to garnish
a mixture of wild rice and basmati rice,
   to serve*

MARINADE:
*4 garlic cloves, peeled
2 fresh cilantro roots
1 tbsp light soy sauce
salt and pepper*

STUFFING:
*4 blades lemongrass
4 kaffir lime leaves
4 slices gingerroot
about 6 tbsp coconut milk, to brush*

1 Wash the chickens and dry on paper towels.

2 Place all the ingredients for the marinade in a small blender and purée until smooth, or grind down in a mortar and pestle. Season to taste with salt and pepper. Rub this marinade mixture into the skin of the chickens, using the back of a spoon to spread it evenly over the skins.

3 Place a blade of lemongrass, a lime leaf and a piece of ginger in the cavity of each chicken.

4 Place the chickens in a roasting pan and brush lightly with the coconut milk. Roast for 30 minutes in the preheated oven.

5 Remove from the oven, brush again with coconut milk, return to the oven and cook for a further 15-25 minutes, until golden and cooked through, depending upon the size of the chickens. The chickens are cooked when the juices from the thigh run clear and are not tinged at all with pink.

6 Serve with the pan juices poured over. Garnish with cilantro leaves and lime wedges.

GREEN CHILI CHICKEN

*The green chili paste gives a hot and spicy flavor to the chicken,
which takes on a vibrant green color.*

STEP 2

STEP 3

STEP 4

STEP 5

SERVES 4

5 tbsp vegetable oil
1 lb boneless chicken breast halves, sliced
    into thin strips
¼ cup coconut milk
3 tbsp brown sugar
3 tsp fish sauce
3 tbsp sliced red and green chilies, seeded
4-6 tbsp chopped fresh basil
3 tbsp thick coconut milk or cream
finely chopped fresh chilies, seeded,
    lemongrass and lemon slices, to garnish

GREEN CURRY PASTE:
2 tsp ground ginger
2 tsp ground cilantro
2 tsp caraway seeds
2 tsp ground nutmeg
2 tsp shrimp paste
2 tsp salt
2 tsp black pepper
pinch of ground cloves
1 stalk lemongrass, finely chopped
2 tbsp chopped cilantro
2 garlic cloves, peeled
2 onions, peeled
grated rind and juice of 2 limes
4 fresh green chilies, about 2 in long, seeded

1 To make the curry paste, place all the ingredients and 2 tablespoons of the oil in a food processor or blender and process to a smooth paste.

2 Heat the remaining oil in a heavy-based saucepan or wok. Add the curry paste and cook for about 30 seconds.

3 Add the chicken strips to the pot and stir-fry over a high heat for about 2-3 minutes.

4 Add the coconut milk, brown sugar, fish sauce and chilies. Cook for 5 minutes, stirring frequently.

5 Remove from the heat, add the basil and toss well to mix.

6 Transfer the chicken to a warmed serving dish. To serve, spoon on a little of the thick coconut milk or cream and garnish with chopped chilies, lemongrass and lemon slices. Serve with steamed or boiled rice.

STEP 1

STEP 2

STEP 3

STEP 4

PEANUT-SESAME CHICKEN

In this quickly prepared dish chicken strips are stir-fried with vegetables. Sesame and peanuts give extra crunch and flavor and the fruit juice glaze gives a shiny coating to the sauce.

SERVES 4

2 tbsp vegetable oil
2 tbsp sesame oil
1 lb boneless, skinned chicken breast halves, sliced into strips
1 1/3 cups broccoli, divided into small flowerets
1/2 lb baby corn, halved if large
1 small red bell pepper, cored, seeded and sliced
2 tbsp soy sauce
1 cup orange juice
2 tsp cornstarch
2 tbsp toasted sesame seeds
1/3 cup roasted, shelled, unsalted peanuts

1 Heat the oils in a large, heavy-based skillet or wok, add the chicken strips and stir-fry until browned, about 4-5 minutes.

2 Add the broccoli, corn and red bell pepper and stir-fry for a further 1-2 minutes.

3 Meanwhile, mix the soy sauce with the orange juice and cornstarch. Stir into the chicken and vegetable mixture, stirring constantly until the sauce has slightly thickened and a glaze develops.

4 Stir in the sesame seeds and peanuts, mixing well. Heat for a further 3-4 minutes, then serve at once, with rice or noodles.

PEANUTS

Make sure you use the unsalted variety of peanuts or the dish will be too salty, because the soy sauce adds saltiness.

CHICKEN & NOODLE ONE-POT

Flavorsome chicken and vegetables cooked with Chinese egg noodles in a coconut sauce. Serve in deep soup bowls.

STEP 1

SERVES 4

1 tbsp sunflower oil
1 onion, sliced
1 garlic clove, crushed
1-in piece gingerroot, peeled and grated
1 bunch scallions, sliced diagonally
1 lb chicken breast fillet, skinned and cut
    into bite-sized pieces
2 tbsp mild curry paste
2 cups coconut milk
1¼ cups chicken stock
salt and pepper
½ lb Chinese egg noodles
2 tsp lime juice
basil sprigs, to garnish

4 Bring to a boil, break the noodles into large pieces, if necessary, add to the pan, cover and simmer for about 6-8 minutes until the noodles are just tender, stirring occasionally.

5 Add the lime juice, taste and adjust the seasoning, if necessary, then serve at once in deep soup bowls.

STEP 2

STEP 3

1 Heat the oil in a wok or large, heavy-based saucepan. Add the onion, garlic, ginger and scallions and stir-fry for 2 minutes until softened.

2 Add the chicken pieces and curry paste and stir-fry until the vegetables and chicken are golden brown, about 4 minutes.

COOK'S TIP

If you enjoy the hot flavors of Thai cooking substitute the mild curry paste in the above recipe with Thai hot curry paste (found in supermarkets and Asian grocery stores) but reduce the quantity to 1 tablespoon.

3 Stir in the coconut milk, stock and salt and pepper to taste, mixing until well blended.

STEP 4

DUCK WITH GINGER & LIME

Just the thing for a lazy summer day – roasted duck breasts sliced and served with a dressing made of ginger, lime juice, sesame oil and fish sauce. Serve on a bed of assorted fresh salad leaves in season.

STEP 1a

STEP 1b

Serves 6
Oven: 400°F

3 boneless duck breasts, about ½ lb each
salt

Dressing:
½ cup olive oil
2 tsp sesame oil
2 tbsp lime juice
grated rind and juice of 1 orange
2 tsp fish sauce
1 tbsp grated gingerroot
1 garlic clove, crushed
2 tsp light soy sauce
3 scallions, finely chopped
1 tsp sugar
about 6 cups assorted salad leaves
orange slices, to garnish, optional

1 Wash the duck breasts, dry on paper towels, then cut in half. Prick the skin all over with a fork and season well with salt. Place the duck pieces, skin-side down, on a wire rack or trivet over a roasting pan. Cook the duck in the preheated oven for 10 minutes then turn over and cook for a further 12-15 minutes, or until the duck is cooked, but still pink in the center, and the skin is crisp.

2 To make the dressing, beat the oils with the lime juice, orange rind and juice, fish sauce, ginger, garlic, soy sauce, scallions, and sugar until well blended.

3 Remove the duck from the oven, allow to cool, then cut into thick slices. Add a little of the dressing to moisten and coat the duck.

4 To serve, arrange assorted salad leaves on a serving dish. Top with the sliced duck breasts and drizzle with the remaining salad dressing.

5 Garnish with orange twists, if using, then serve at once.

STEP 2

COOK'S TIP

If an extra crisp skin is preferred on the duck, quickly fry the duck breasts, skin-side down, in a nonstick pan (without any additional oil) for a few minutes until golden. Cook in the oven as above, but reduce the cooking time by about 3 minutes.

STEP 3

STEP 1

STEP 2

STEP 3a

STEP 3b

BEEF & BOK CHOY

A colorful selection of vegetables stir-fried with tender strips of steak.

SERVES 4

1 large head of bok choy, torn into large
  pieces
2 tbsp vegetable oil
2 garlic cloves, crushed
1 lb sirloin or filet mignon, cut into thin
  strips
1 cup snow peas, trimmed
16-18 baby corn
6 scallions, chopped
2 red bell peppers, cored, seeded and thinly
  sliced
2 tbsp oyster sauce
1 tbsp fish sauce
1 tbsp sugar

1 Steam the bok choy leaves over boiling water until just tender. Keep warm.

2 Heat the oil in a large, heavy-based skillet or wok, add the garlic and steak strips and stir-fry until just browned, about 1-2 minutes.

3 Add the snow peas, baby corn, scallions, red bell pepper, oyster sauce, fish sauce and sugar to the skillet, mixing well. Stir-fry for a further 2-3 minutes until the vegetables are just tender, but still crisp.

4 Arrange the bok choy leaves in the base of a heated serving dish and spoon the beef and vegetable mixture into the center.

5 Serve the stir-fry immediately, with rice or noodles.

VARIATION

Bok choy is one of the most important ingredients in this dish. It is a variety of Chinese cabbage and it has a mild flavor similar to cabbage. You will also find it called Chinese mustard or pak choy or pak choi.

GREEN BEEF CURRY

This is a quickly-made curry prepared with strips of beef steak, cubed eggplant and onion in a cream sauce flavored with green curry paste. Serve with fluffy rice and a salad.

SERVES 4

1 eggplant, peeled and cubed
2 onions, cut into thin wedges
2 tbsp vegetable oil
Green Curry Paste (see page 37)
1 lb beef tenderloin, cut into thin strips
2 cups thick coconut milk or cream
2 tbsp fish sauce
1 tbsp brown sugar
1 red chili, seeded and very finely chopped
1 green chili, seeded and very finely chopped
1-in piece gingerroot, finely chopped
4 kaffir lime leaves, torn into pieces
chopped fresh basil, to garnish

1 Blanch the eggplant cubes and onion wedges in boiling water for about 2 minutes, to soften. Drain thoroughly.

2 Heat the oil in a large heavy-based saucepan or wok, add the curry paste and cook for 1 minute.

3 Add the beef strips and stir-fry, over a high heat, for about 1 minute, to brown on all sides.

4 Add the coconut milk or cream, fish sauce and sugar to the pot and bring the mixture to a boil, stirring constantly.

5 Add the eggplant and onion, chilies, ginger and lime leaves. Cook for a further 2 minutes.

6 Sprinkle with chopped basil to serve. Accompany with rice.

COCONUT MILK

Coconut milk is sold in cans, or you can make your own. Pour 1¼ cups boiling water over 2½ cups shredded coconut and simmer over low heat for 30 minutes. Strain the milk into a bowl through a piece of cheesecloth. Gather the ends of cheesecloth together and squeeze tightly to extract as much liquid as possible.

STEP 1

STEP 2

STEP 4

STEP 5

PEPPERED BEEF & CASHEWS

A simple but stunning dish of tender strips of beef mixed with crunchy cashew nuts, coated in a hot sauce. Serve with rice noodles.

SERVES 4

1 tbsp peanut or sunflower oil
1 tbsp sesame oil
1 onion, sliced
1 garlic clove, crushed
1 tbsp grated gingerroot
1 lb filet mignon or sirloin, cut into thin
    strips
2 tsp palm or dark brown sugar
2 tbsp light soy sauce
1 small yellow bell pepper, cored, seeded and
    sliced
1 red bell pepper, cored, seeded and sliced
4 scallions, chopped
2 celery stalks, chopped
4 large open-cap mushrooms, sliced
4 tbsp roasted cashew nuts
3 tbsp stock or white wine

1 Heat the oils in a large, heavy-based skillet or wok. Add the onion, garlic and ginger and stir-fry for about 2 minutes until softened and lightly colored.

2 Add the steak strips and stir-fry for a further 2-3 minutes until the meat has browned.

3 Add the sugar and soy sauce, mixing well.

4 Add the bell peppers, scallions, celery, mushrooms and cashews, mixing well.

5 Add the stock or wine and stir-fry for 2-3 minutes until the beef is cooked through and the vegetables are tender-crisp.

6 Serve the stir-fry immediately with rice noodles.

PALM SUGAR

Palm sugar is a thick brown sugar with a slightly caramel taste. It is sold in cakes, or in small containers. If not available, use soft dark brown sugar.

GARLIC, PORK & SHRIMP

This is a wonderful one-pot dish of stir-fried pork tenderloin with shrimp and noodles that is made in minutes.
Serve straight from the pan.

STEP 1

SERVES 4

½ lb medium Chinese egg noodles
3 tbsp vegetable oil
2 garlic cloves, crushed
12 oz pork tenderloin, cut into strips
⅓ cup dried shrimp, or 4 oz shelled, raw shrimp
1 bunch scallions, finely chopped
¾ cup chopped roasted and shelled unsalted peanuts
3 tbsp fish sauce
1½ tsp palm or dark brown sugar
1-2 small red chilies, seeded and finely chopped (to taste)
3 tbsp lime juice
3 tbsp chopped fresh cilantro
cilantro sprigs, to garnish

1 Place the noodles in a large saucepan of boiling water, then immediately remove from the heat. Cover and leave to stand for 6 minutes, stirring once halfway through the time. At the end of 6 minutes the noodles will be perfectly cooked. Alternatively, follow the package instructions. Drain the noodles thoroughly and keep warm.

2 Heat the oil in a large, heavy-based saucepan or wok, add the garlic

STEP 2

and pork and stir-fry until the pork strips are browned, about 2-3 minutes.

3 Add the dried shrimp or shelled shrimp, scallions, peanuts, fish sauce, sugar, chilies to taste and lime juice. Stir-fry for a further 1 minute.

4 Add the cooked noodles and cilantro and stir-fry until heated through, about 1 minute. Serve the stir-fry immediately, garnished with cilantro sprigs. If you prefer, the dish can be prepared with rice as an accompaniment rather than adding in the noodles.

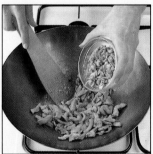

STEP 3

FISH SAUCE

Fish sauce is made from pressed, salted fish and is available in some supermarkets and Oriental stores. It is very salty, so no extra salt should be added.

STEP 4

CHAPTER FOUR

Accompaniments

Good Thai food is a happy marriage of many different dishes that contrast in flavor, color and texture. Rice may well be the staple food, but freshly cooked plain long-grain rice is only one way of serving this basic. In countless other dishes it is baked, steamed, stir-fried and boiled with an almost infinite spectrum of vegetables, herbs, spices and flavorings to entice and delight.

Noodles also have a major role to play when snacks come to the fore. Many noodles, fried with just a few extra ingredients, make superb light meals to enjoy in their own right. No self-respecting Thai would do without the bowl of midday noodles!

The Thais also employ clever ways with their rich supply of vegetables, such as shallots, garlic, baby corn, cabbage, green beans, broccoli, bell peppers and mushrooms. Sliced and diced they are used in imaginative stir-fries; cubed and sliced they are braised in aromatic broths and sauces; and finely shredded they make exciting, palate-tingling salads with exotic dressings made from limes, fish sauce, ginger, soy sauce and sesame oil.

Opposite: *A basket stall in the floating market in Bangkok.*

THAI SALAD

This is a typical Thai-style salad made by mixing fruit and vegetables with the sharp, sweet and fishy flavors of the dressing.

STEP 1

STEP 2

STEP 3

STEP 4

SERVES 4-6

4¹/₂ cups white cabbage, finely shredded
2 tomatoes, skinned, seeded and chopped
1¹/₂ cups cooked green beans, halved if large
4 oz shelled raw shrimp
1 papaya, peeled, seeded and chopped
1-2 fresh red chilies, seeded and very finely
    sliced
scant ¹/₃ cup roasted salted peanuts, crushed
handful of lettuce or baby spinach leaves,
    shredded or torn into small pieces
cilantro sprigs, to garnish

DRESSING:
4 tbsp lime juice
2 tbsp fish sauce
sugar, to taste
pepper

3 To make the dressing, beat the lime juice with the fish sauce and add sugar and pepper to taste. Drizzle over the salad.

4 Scatter the top with the remaining papaya, chilies and crushed peanuts. Garnish with cilantro leaves and serve at once.

1 Mix the cabbage with the tomatoes, green beans, shrimp, three-quarters of the papaya and half the chilies in a bowl. Stir in two-thirds of the crushed peanuts and mix well.

2 Line the rim of a large serving plate with the lettuce or spinach and pile the salad mixture into the center.

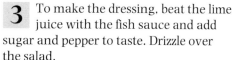

SKINNING TOMATOES

To skin tomatoes, make a cross at the base with a very sharp knife, then immerse in a bowl of boiling water for a few minutes. Remove with a slotted spoon and peel off the skin.

FRAGRANT THAI COCONUT RICE

This is the finest rice to serve with Thai-style food. Basmati rice is cooked with creamed coconut, lemongrass, fresh ginger and spices to make a wonderfully aromatic, fluffy rice.

STEP 1

SERVES 4-6

1-in piece gingerroot, peeled and sliced
2 cloves
1 piece lemongrass, bruised and halved
2 tsp ground nutmeg
1 cinnamon stick
1 bay leaf
2 small thin strips lime rind
1 tsp salt
2 tbsp creamed coconut, chopped
2½ cups water
1¾ cups basmati rice
ground pepper

LEMONGRASS

When using a whole stem of lemongrass (rather than chopped lemongrass), beat it well to bruise it so that the flavor is fully released. Lemon rind can be used instead.

STEP 2a

1 Place the ginger, cloves, lemongrass, nutmeg, cinnamon stick, bay leaf, lime rind, salt, creamed coconut and water in a large, heavy-based saucepan and bring slowly to a boil.

2 Add the rice, stir well, then cover and simmer, over a very gentle heat, for about 15 minutes or until all the liquid has been absorbed and the rice is tender but still has a bite to it.

COOKING RICE

An alternative method of cooking the rice – the absorption method – leaves you free to concentrate on other dishes. Add the rice to the pan as in step 1, then bring back to a boil. Stir well, then cover tightly and turn off the heat. Leave for 20-25 minutes before removing the lid – the rice will be perfectly cooked.

STEP 2b

3 Remove from the heat, add pepper to taste, then fluff up the rice with a fork. Remove the large pieces of spices before serving.

STEP 3

SESAME HOT NOODLES

Plain egg noodles are all the better when tossed in a dressing made with nutty sesame oil, soy sauce, peanut butter, cilantro, lime juice, chili and sesame seeds. Serve hot as a main meal accompaniment.

STEP 1

SERVES 6

1 lb medium Chinese egg noodles
3 tbsp sunflower oil
2 tbsp sesame oil
1 garlic clove, crushed
1 tbsp smooth peanut butter
1 small green chili, seeded and very finely
   chopped
3 tbsp toasted sesame seeds
4 tbsp light soy sauce
1-2 tbsp lime juice
salt and pepper
4 tbsp chopped fresh cilantro

1 Place the noodles in a large saucepan of boiling water, then immediately remove from the heat. Cover and leave to stand for 6 minutes, stirring once halfway through the time. At the end of 6 minutes the noodles will be perfectly cooked. Otherwise follow the package instructions.

2 Meanwhile, to make the dressing, mix the oils with the garlic and peanut butter until smooth.

3 Add the chili, sesame seeds, soy sauce and lime juice, according to taste and mix well. Season with salt and pepper.

4 Drain the noodles thoroughly, then place in a heated serving bowl. Add the dressing and cilantro and toss well to mix. Serve immediately.

STEP 2

STEP 3

COOKING NOODLES

If you are cooking noodles ahead of time, toss the cooked, drained noodles in 2 teaspoons sesame oil, then turn into a bowl. Cover and keep warm.

STEP 4

STEP 2

STEP 3

STEP 4a

STEP 4b

THAI FRIED RICE

*The Thais often serve their rice fried, but not just plain and simple –
they give theirs an extra punch and bit of a zip with hot red chilies,
scallions and fish sauce.*

SERVES 4

1¼ cup basmati rice
3 tbsp sunflower oil
1 hot red chili, seeded and finely chopped
2 tsp fish sauce
3 scallions chopped
1 large egg, beaten
1 tbsp chopped parsley or cilantro
1 tbsp soy sauce
1 tsp sugar
salt and pepper

1 Cook the rice in boiling salted water until tender, about 10 minutes. Drain, rinse with boiling water and drain again thoroughly. Spread out on a large plate or baking sheet to dry.

2 Heat the oil in a large, heavy-based skillet or wok until hot. Add the chili, fish sauce and scallions and stir-fry for 1-2 minutes.

3 Add the beaten egg and stir-fry quickly so that the egg scrambles into small fluffy pieces.

4 Fork through the rice to separate the grains, then add to the skillet and stir-fry for about 1 minute to mix and heat through.

5 Sprinkle a little of the chopped parsley or cilantro over the rice. Mix the soy sauce with the sugar and remaining chopped parsley or cilantro and stir into the rice mixture, tossing well to mix. Season to taste. Serve immediately.

FRIED RICE

For perfect fried rice it is important that the rice is thoroughly dry and cool before it is added to the pan, otherwise it may become lumpy and soggy.

THAI BRAISED VEGETABLES

This colorful selection of braised vegetables makes a splendid accompaniment to a main dish.

STEP 1

SERVES 4-6

3 tbsp sunflower oil
1 garlic clove, crushed
1 Chinese cabbage, thickly shredded
2 onions, peeled and cut into wedges
1⅓ cups broccoli flowerets
2 large carrots, peeled and cut into thin
    julienne strips
12 baby corn, halved if large
⅓ cup snow peas, halved
1¼ cups Chinese or oyster mushrooms,
    sliced
1 tbsp grated gingerroot
¾ cup vegetable stock
2 tbsp light soy sauce
1 tbsp cornstarch
salt and pepper
½ tsp sugar

1 Heat the oil in a large, heavy-based skillet or wok. Add the garlic, cabbage, onions, broccoli, carrots, corn, snow peas, mushrooms and ginger and stir-fry for 2 minutes.

2 Add the stock, cover and cook for a further 2-3 minutes.

3 Blend the soy sauce with the cornstarch and salt and pepper to taste.

4 Remove the braised vegetables from the pan with a slotted spoon and keep warm. Add the soy sauce mixture to the skillet juices, mixing well. Bring to a boil, stirring constantly, until the mixture thickens slightly. Stir in the sugar.

5 Return the vegetables to the pan and toss in the slightly thickened sauce. Cook gently to just heat through, then serve immediately.

STEP 2

STEP 3

VARIATION

This dish also makes an ideal vegetarian main meal. Double the quantities, to serve 4-6, and serve with noodles or Thai Fried Rice (page 60).

STEP 5

CHAPTER FIVE

Desserts

Few things are more beguiling and enticing than a stunning array
of mixed tropical fruits carefully arranged on a platter to round
off a meal, and the Thais make this traditional dessert an art form:
slices of sunset-colored mango and papaya nestle against
jewel-like green and black disks of kiwi fruit, wheels of
fragrant yellow pineapple and diagonally
sliced strips of banana.

Desserts, as Westerners know them, usually only appear at
banquets and special festive occasions, although sweet treats can
be bought from street vendors on almost every corner.

When it is time to celebrate the Thais use their wealth of tropical
fruits to make superb fruit salads, stuffed pancakes, wontons and
baby dumplings. They use rice to make a rich and creamy
pudding baked with coconut milk, and purée fruits to make
ice creams, parfaits and exotic water ices. The all-time favorite is
Thai-style Bananas, sliced and cooked in butter with orange rind,
sugar and lime juice, flamed with orange-flavored
liqueur and sprinkled with toasted coconut shreds, all the better
for serving with a dollop of coconut-flavored cream
or ice cream. No wonder the Thais save it for best!

Opposite: *A street vendor in
Bangkok displays her fruit on
banana leaves, often used to
wrap and bake fish. The
leaves are inedible, but impart
a delicate flavor to the
cooked fish.*

THAI-STYLE BANANAS

The Thais rarely finish a meal with an elaborate dessert, preferring to eat a selection of tropical fruits. This is one of the exceptions and after tasting it, you will understand why.

STEP 1

Serves 6

3 tbsp shredded fresh coconut
1/4 cup sweet butter
1 tbsp grated gingerroot
grated rind of 1 orange
6 bananas
1/4 cup sugar
4 tbsp fresh lime juice
6 tbsp orange liqueur (Cointreau or Grand
   Marnier, for example)
3 tsp toasted sesame seeds
lime slices, to decorate
ice cream, to serve (optional)

1 Heat a small nonstick skillet until hot. Add the coconut and cook, stirring constantly, for about 1 minute until lightly colored. Remove from the skillet and allow to cool.

2 Melt the butter in the skillet until it melts. Add the ginger and orange rind and mix well.

3 Peel and slice the bananas lengthwise (and halve if they are very large). Place the bananas cut-side down in the butter mixture and cook for 1-2 minutes or until the sauce mixture starts to become sticky. Turn to coat in the sauce.

4 Remove the bananas from the skillet and place on heated serving plates. Keep warm.

5 Return the pan to the heat and add the orange liqueur, stirring well to blend. Ignite with a taper, allow the flames to die down, then pour over the bananas.

6 Sprinkle with the coconut and sesame seeds and serve at once, decorated with slices of lime.

STEP 2

STEP 3

VARIATION

For a very special treat serve this with a flavored ice cream, such as coconut, ginger or praline.

STEP 5

STEP 1

STEP 3a

STEP 3b

STEP 5

MANGO PARFAIT

This is a beautifully soft parfait that can be served straight from the freezer. Serve with crisp dessert cookies or, when time and the waistline allows, with deep-fried, sugar-dusted wontons.

SERVES 4

1 large ripe mango
juice of 1 lime
about 1 tbsp sugar
3 egg yolks
½ cup confectioners' sugar, sifted
⅔ cup heavy cream
lime rind, to decorate
fried wonton skins dusted with sugar, to
    serve (optional)

1 Peel the mango and slice the flesh away from the seed. Purée in a food processor or blender with the lime juice and sugar to taste until the mixture is smooth.

2 Beat the egg yolks with the confectioners' sugar until the mixture is pale and thick, then fold in the mango purée.

3 Whip the cream until it stands in soft peaks. Fold into the mango mixture with a metal spoon.

4 Pour the mango mixture into 4 freezerproof serving glasses and freeze until firm, about 4-6 hours.

5 Serve the parfaits straight from the freezer (they will be soft enough to scoop) with crisp dessert cookies or warm fried wontons (see instructions below) dusted with sugar.

FRIED WONTONS

Allow about 2 wonton skins per person, which you can buy in packages at Chinese or other Asian grocery stores. Deep-fry the wonton skins in hot oil for about 30 seconds until crisp and golden. Drain on paper towels, then dust with confectioners' sugar to serve.

STEP 1

STEP 2

STEP 3a

STEP 3b

BAKED COCONUT-RICE PUDDING

A wonderful baked rice pudding cooked with flavorsome coconut milk and a little lime rind. Serve hot or chilled with fresh or stewed fruit.

SERVES 4-6
OVEN: 325°F

$^1/_3$ cup short-grain or round-grain pudding
    rice
$2^1/_2$ cups coconut milk
$1^1/_4$ cups milk
1 large strip lime rind
$^1/_4$ cup sugar
knob of butter
pinch of ground star anise (optional)
fresh or stewed fruit, to serve

1 Mix the rice with the coconut milk, milk, lime rind and sugar.

2 Pour the rice mixture into a lightly-greased 5-cup shallow ovenproof dish and dot the surface with a little butter. Bake in the oven for about 30 minutes.

3 Remove the mixture from the oven and discard the strip of lime. Stir the pudding well, add the pinch of ground star anise, if using, return to the oven and cook for a further 1-2 hours or until almost all the milk has been absorbed and a golden brown skin has baked on the top of the pudding. Cover the top of the pudding with foil if it starts to brown too much toward the end of the cooking time.

4 Serve the pudding warm or chilled with fresh or stewed fruit.

COOK'S TIP

As the mixture cools it thickens. If you plan to serve the rice chilled, fold in about 3 tbsp cream or extra coconut milk before serving to give a thinner consistency.

STEP 1

STEP 2a

STEP 2b

STEP 5

FRUIT SALAD WITH GINGER SYRUP

This is a very special fruit salad made from the most exotic and colorful fruits that are soaked in a syrup made with fresh ginger.

SERVES 6-8

1-in piece gingerroot, peeled and chopped
$^1/_4$ cup sugar
$^2/_3$ cup water
grated rind and juice of 1 lime
$^1/_3$ cup ginger wine
1 fresh pineapple, peeled, cored and cut into
    bite-sized pieces
2 ripe mangoes, peeled, seeded and diced
4 kiwi fruit, peeled and sliced
1 papaya, peeled, seeded and diced
2 passion fruit, halved and flesh removed
12 oz lychees, peeled and pitted
$^1/_4$ fresh coconut, grated
2 oz Cape gooseberries, to decorate
    (optional)
coconut ice cream, to serve (optional)

1 Place the ginger, sugar, water and lime juice in a small saucepan and bring slowly to a boil. Simmer for 1 minute, remove from the heat and allow the syrup to cool slightly.

2 Pass the sugar syrup through a fine strainer, then add the ginger wine and mix well. Allow to cool completely.

3 Place the prepared pineapple, mango, kiwi, papaya, passion fruit and lychees in a serving bowl. Add the cold syrup and mix well. Cover and chill for 2-4 hours.

4 Just before serving, add half of the grated coconut to the salad and mix well. Sprinkle the remainder on the top of the fruit salad.

5 If using Cape gooseberries to decorate the fruit salad, peel back each calyx to form a flower. Wipe the berries with a damp cloth, then arrange them around the side of the fruit salad before serving.

GINGER WINE

This is a sweet, ginger-flavored wine that is often drunk as an aperitif. Do not confuse this with ginger ale. If you can not find any, substitute sweet sherry.

PANCAKES POLAMAI

These Thai pancakes are filled with an exotic array of tropical fruits.
Decorate lavishly with tropical flowers or mint sprigs.

STEP 1

STEP 2

STEP 3

SERVES 4

BATTER:
1 cup all-purpose flour
pinch of salt
1 egg
1 egg yolk
1¼ cups coconut milk
4 tsp vegetable oil, plus oil for frying

FILLING:
1 banana
1 papaya
juice of 1 lime
2 passion fruit
1 mango, peeled, seeded and sliced
4 lychees, pitted and halved
1-2 tbsp honey
flowers or mint sprigs, to decorate

1 To make the batter, sift the flour into a bowl with the salt. Make a well in the center, add the egg and egg yolk and a little of the coconut milk. Gradually draw the flour into the egg mixture, beating well and gradually adding the remaining coconut milk to make a smooth batter. Add the oil and mix well. Cover and chill for 30 minutes.

2 To make the filling, peel and slice the banana and place in a bowl.

Peel and slice the papaya, remove and discard the seeds, then cut into bite-sized chunks. Add to the banana with the lime juice and mix well to coat.

3 Cut the passion fruit in half and scoop out the flesh and seeds into the fruit bowl. Add the mango, lychees and honey and mix well.

4 To make the pancakes, heat a little oil in a 6-in pancake pan or skillet. Pour in just enough of the pancake batter to cover the base of the pan and tilt so it spreads thinly and evenly. Cook until the pancake is just set and the underside is lightly browned, turn and briefly cook the other side. Remove from the pan and keep warm. Repeat with the remaining batter to make a total of 8 pancakes.

5 To serve, place a little of the prepared fruit filling along the center of each pancake and then, using both hands, roll it into a cone shape. Lay seam-side down on warmed serving plates, allowing 2 pancakes per serving.

6 Serve the stuffed pancakes at once, decorated with flowers and mint sprigs, if liked.

STEP 4

THAI COOKING

COOKING EQUIPMENT AND METHODS

In Thailand, there are few gas and electric ovens or broilers as Westerners know them, so most cooking is done on an open charcoal stove. Meat and fish are frequently barbecued or broiled and woks are set upon their surfaces to stir-fry, boil, steam or simmer dishes. A wok is therefore the most necessary piece of equipment required for cooking - although a heavy-duty, deep skillet may suffice. There is really very little need for specialist equipment, although the following special items may be worth the investment to the avid Thai cook:

Mortar and Pestle An absolute must to crush spices, herbs and other flavorings to make pastes for flavoring a whole host of dishes. A small electric herb grinder or coffee grinder, specifically reserved for spices, could be employed instead and it does cut down on the elbow grease!

Steamer A steamer, with a good tight-fitting lid, is necessary to cook foods gently above boiling water. Chinese bamboo steamers are ideal solutions at very little cost and can be purchased cheaply from Chinese supermarkets. An improvised set-up could use a metal colander over a saucepan with tight-fitting lid to cover.

continued opposite

Thailand has a richly abundant and totally unique cuisine that has changed little over the centuries, despite regular foreign intervention. Today, it still stands independent, with head held high, to critical gastronomic scrutiny and fares the better for it.

It is not difficult to spot the influence of near neighbors like China and India in stir-fries and curries but somehow they are given the unmistakeable Thai treatment with herbs, spices and coconut milk. So it is easy to see how on the one hand Thai cuisine can be described as light, aromatic and zestful, yet on the other hot, handsome, robust and full-blooded!

Thai cuisine is dependent upon the rich harvests of rice, green vegetables, herbs, spices and fruit. A lavish supply of fish means that normally at least one fish dish, be it sizzling shrimp, a fish curry or banana-wrapped baked whole fish, features in every Thai meal. Meat, of all types, also makes for a varied cuisine where there are few, if any, religious restrictions to the basic diet.

Rice is the staple food and is served at every meal with many main-course meat, fish, poultry and vegetable dishes in a sauce. Noodles are generally served as snack or "fast" foods to supplement the main meal. Soups also feature frequently and are typically flavored with Thai staples like lemongrass, lime juice and fish sauce.

Creamy curries, ranging from mild and aromatic to fierce and fiery, are prepared daily with care from some of the finest fresh ingredients and spicy curry pastes whose bases are red or green chili peppers.

SPECIAL INGREDIENTS

Such has been the popularity of Thai food that many supermarkets boast the ingredients required to cook a Thai meal. Only a few special foods will have to be purchased from specialist and Oriental food stores and, fortunately, these seem to be less obscure than they once were.

Bamboo shoots Still only available canned and sometimes dried (which need soaking before use), bamboo shoots are the crunchy, cream-colored shoots of the bamboo plant.

Banana leaves These are the large green, inedible leaves of the banana tree that are principally used for wrapping food and for making containers for steaming purposes. They give the food a slightly aromatic delicate flavor but cannot be eaten.

Basil Holy basil or Thai basil, available from specialist stores, has a stronger, more pungent and sharper flavor than our Mediterranean or "sweet" basil. When unavailable, use ordinary basil in the same proportions.

Bean sauce A thick sauce made from yellow or black soybeans. The crushed beans are mixed with flour, vinegar, spices and salt to make a spicy, sometimes salty and definitely aromatic sauce. It is usually sold in cans or jars.

Bean sprouts The tiny, crunchy shoots of mung beans. These are widely available fresh and should be used on the day of purchase. Canned bean sprouts are available but generally lack flavor and crunchiness.

Chili paste This is a paste of roast ground chilies mixed with oil. Depending upon the chilies used, the color and flavor will differ appreciably so only add a small amount to err on the side of safety. It is sold in plastic tubes, small jars and may be called "ground chilies in oil". A small amount will last a long time if stored in the refrigerator.

Fresh chilies Fresh chilies come in varying degrees of hotness. Cooking helps to mellow the flavor but a degree of caution should be exercised when using them. If you do not like your food too hot discard the seeds when you prepare them. Remember, at all costs, to make sure that you wash your hands thoroughly after touching chilies because they contain an irritant which will sting the eyes and mouth harshly on contact. Fresh chopped hot chilies can be replaced with chili paste or cayenne pepper but the result will be slightly different. As a general guide for buying – the smaller the chili the hotter it will be. Most supermarkets stock the larger, milder chili and this is perhaps the best starting point for the novice Thai cook.

Dried chilies These add a surprisingly good kick to a dish, especially if they are tossed in oil with other spices at the beginning of cooking. Generally the chilies are added whole but can sometimes be halved. In most cases they should be removed from the dish before serving. Again, the smaller the dried chili, the hotter the flavor.

Cilantro This is a delicate and fragrant herb that is widely used in Thai cooking. The roots and the leaves are used, the former having a more intense flavor. The roots are generally used for cooking and the leaves are used more for flavoring the cooked and finished dish. Chopped leaves are frequently stirred into a cooked dish or scattered over the surface just prior to serving.

Coconut Fresh coconut is used in a good many sweet and savory Thai dishes and is infinitely better to use than shredded coconut. Many supermarkets now stock them fresh at little cost.

Coconut milk Coconut milk is an infusion used to flavor and thicken many Thai dishes. Perhaps the best and easiest type to use comes in cans from Oriental stores but remember to check that it is unsweetened for savory dishes.

Curry leaves Rather like bay leaves but not quite so thick and luscious, these are highly aromatic leaves that are chopped, torn or left whole and added to many Thai curries and slow-simmered dishes. Olive green in color, these can be bought fresh or dried from specialist shops.

Cooking Equipment & Methods cont.
Wok A large skillet can be used instead of this special pan with distinctive sloping and rounded edges, but devotees will tell you how useful it is not only for stir-frying but also for deep-frying, steaming, boiling, and stewing foods.

PREPARING A FRESH COCONUT

When buying a coconut choose one that is heavy for its size. To open it, pierce the "eyes" with a skewer and pour away the liquid. Heating the coconut in the oven will help with further preparation - place in a preheated moderately hot oven, 375°F, for about 10-15 minutes, then place on the floor or a sturdy surface and give it a sharp tap with a mallet or hammer. The coconut should cleanly break in half. The flesh can then be prised away with a sharp knife from the shell. The brown skin can then be peeled from the white flesh. Cut the flesh into pieces or grate as required, by hand or in a food processor to use as required. Grated fresh coconut and coconut pieces freeze well for up to 2 months.

FRESH COCONUT MILK

To make it from fresh grated coconut, place about 1½ cups grated coconut in a bowl, pour over about 2½ cups of boiling water to just cover and leave to stand for 1 hour. Strain through cheesecloth, squeezing hard to extract as much "thick" milk as possible. If you require coconut cream then leave to stand, then skim the "cream" from the surface for use. Unsweetened shredded coconut can also be used in the same quantities.

TAMARIND WATER

Tamarind is the dried fruit of the tamarind tree that has a sharp, acidic taste. The pods are used as a souring agent. Sold as pods or pulp they must be made into tamarind water to use. To do this you have to soak 1 oz pulp in 1¼ cups hot water, stir well and leave for about 20 minutes. The water is then strained off, pressing as much as possible from the pulp. Tamarind paste or concentrate is available from specialist stores and is ready to use. It is simply mixed with stock or water or added directly to the dish. Use according to the package or recipe instructions. Vinegar or lemon juice in water can be used instead but they make a poor alternative. Tamarind is one of the ingredients that gives Thai cuisine its special sweet-and-sour flavor.

Fish paste This is a thick fish paste made from fermented fish or shrimp and salt. It is used only in small amounts since it has enormous flavoring power. Anchovy paste makes a good if not authentic alternative.

Fish sauce/Nam pla This is a thin, brown salty sauce that is widely used in Thai cooking instead of salt. It is made by pressing salted fish and is available in many Oriental food stores. There is really no good available substitute so is worth hunting for.

Galangal Galangal is a spice very similar to ginger and is used to replace the latter in Thai cuisine. It can be bought fresh from Oriental food stores but is also available dried and as a powder. The fresh root, which is not as pungent as ginger, needs to be peeled before slicing to use, while dried pieces need to be soaked in water before using and discarded from the dish before serving. If fresh galangal is unavailable for a recipe, substitute 1 dried slice or 1 teaspoon powder for each ½ in fresh.

Gingerroot This is also often used in Thai cooking. Always peel before using, then chop, grate or purée to a paste to use. Buy gingerroot in small quantities to ensure freshness and store in a plastic bag in the refrigerator.

Kaffir lime leaves These are dark green, glossy leaves that have a lemony-lime flavor that can be bought from specialist shops either fresh or dried. Fresh leaves impart the most delicious flavor to a dish so they are worth seeking out. Most recipes call for the leaves to be left whole or shredded. This is best done with a pair of scissors. When stocks cannot be found, substitute 1 leaf with about 1 teaspoon finely grated lime rind.

Lemongrass Known also as citronelle, lemongrass is a tropical grass with a pungent, aromatic lemon flavor. It is fairly easy to buy fresh from large supermarkets. When chopped lemongrass is specified then use the thick bulky end of the scallion like stalk. Alternatively, if the whole stalk is required beat well to bruise so that the flavor can be imparted. Stalks keep well in the refrigerator for up to about 2 weeks. When unavailable used grated lemon rind instead or a pared piece of lemon rind. Dried lemongrass is also available as a powder called *sereh*.

Noodles Many, many different varieties.

Oyster sauce Oriental oyster sauce, a light sauce made from oysters and soy sauce, is frequently used as a flavoring in Thai cooking. It is often used to flavor meat and vegetables during cooking. Despite its name, oyster sauce, it is entirely free from the flavor of oysters, or indeed fish!

Palm sugar This is a thick, coarse brown sugar that has a slightly caramel taste. It is sold in round cakes or in small round, flat containers. It is not strictly necessary and can be replaced with dark soft brown sugar.

Rice Check your recipe to see whether you require long-grain fragrant Thai rice or a "sticky" glutinous rice before preparation. Most recipes call for the long-grain fragrant variety labeled as Thai but when unavailable then replace with a good-quality basmati or other long-grain rice. When the shorter, stickier rice is required, opt for Italian, arborio or medium round-grain rice. Wash both types very well before use until the water runs clear. This gets rid of any dirt, dust and starch which can ruin the final appearance of the dish.

Rice vinegar This is vinegar made from rice but with a far less acidic flavor than Western varieties. Cider vinegar makes a good alternative.

Sesame oil A nutty-flavored oil, generally used in small quantities at the end of cooking for flavor. Sometimes sesame oil is used with peanut or sunflower oil for stir-frying.

Shrimp paste Thai shrimp paste is a dark brown, dry paste made from shrimp and salt and is used in small amounts to flavor sauces. Anchovy paste makes a good substitute.

Shrimp, dried These are strongly-flavored dried shrimp available whole or in powder form. Whole ones should be rinsed before use.

Soy sauce Choose from light and dark types. The light variety, difficult to find, is light in color but saltier in taste and still full of flavor. It is the best type to use in cooking. The dark variety is darker in color and often a little thicker than the light type. It is more generally used as a condiment or dipping sauce.

Star anise A Chinese spice with a distinctive licorice flavor. It is a spice that is shaped like a star with eight points and is used to flavor meat and poultry dishes in particular.

Tofu Also called bean curd, this is a food made from puréed and pressed soybeans. It is sold with several textures: extra-firm, firm and soft, called silken. Most is plain and bland although some specialist health-food stores sell the smoked variety. It is highly nutritious and does take on the flavor of the things it is being cooked with. The type used for stir-frying should be firm so that it does not crumble during cooking, and is best cut into cubes for use. Don't be tempted to overmix or stir too vigorously during preparation. A very good ingredient for sweet and savory dishes – ideal, too, for vegetarian dishes.

Water chestnuts Only available in cans but quite acceptable. These give a lovely crunch to a stir-fry, salad or vegetable accompaniment.

Wonton skins These are thin, yellow squares of dough generally packed in cellophane for easy use. Store in the refigerator before use and do not allow to dry out or they will become dry and brittle and unsuitable for wrapping around sweet and savory mixtures that are steamed or fried. Filo pastry makes a good alternative when unavailable.

CREAMED COCONUT

Look for bars of creamed coconut in Asian grocery stores. It can be used to make coconut milk. Follow the package instruction, or, as a general guide, grate 3 oz creamed coconut into ¾ cup hot water and stir well to blend. The milk made by this method is often very rich and creamy.

NOODLES

Many different varieties of noodles are used in Thai cooking and most can be bought fresh or dried from supermarkets and specialist stores. Most are inter-changeable in recipes but the type stated is probably the best to choose. Choose from rice noodles or sticks, medium-flat rice noodles, rice vermicelli or very thin rice noodles, egg noodles and "cellophane" or very thin transparent noodles. Dried noodles need to be soaked in cold water before using during which time they double their weight. They then require only a very short cooking time. Fresh noodles do not require any precooking and they are cooked in the same way as the presoaked dried variety.

INDEX